Published By Lift Bridge Publishing

ISBN-13: 979-8-88567-792-9

Glass Door

Vision from Heaven

Table of Content

Introduction

This book is a journey of self-discovery.

I discovered myself and my gifts through God who is always there talking, guiding, and showing me what to do. I just did not know how to listen and or completely understand what I was being shown. I had to grow and unlearn a lot of worldly views habits and ways to walk in God's fullness. To surrender and trust him in all his ways. There are always new levels in him to discover and I am here for the ride.

Your identity or who you think you are here in this material realm is not who you really are. You are not, none of those superficial things this world deems important. The real you is directly connected to the energy force/source (God) that created you and the entire universe.

Thank you to the creator of the universe (God) for sending me what I needed when I needed it. Thank you to the ear you put it in to deliver it to me to grow push and pull me (My Wonderful Pastors). You knew what I needed when I wasn't even looking for it or understood how to receive it! You held my hand in the dark and pulled me out into the light and directly into you! I love you!

3 am Prayer & Worship

While sleeping on Monday morning my mind was on Christ. I sang myself to sleep with the TV on the music station. I was up but not up, around 3 am in that in-between sleep & wake place. In prayer and worship, thanking God, speaking in tongues. As well as casting the enemy out of my house. While in the midst of it, I see faces. First, a young girl maybe in her late-teens sitting under a street light with her back against a wall, with her knees up and her arms wrapped around her knees. She had a very pretty round caramel face round nose medium-length hair. She turns and looks at me as if I was right there with her.

I suddenly hear Pastor Portia say, pray for her. We talked and I prayed with her and for her for what seemed like hours. Then I was somewhere else, and then a man appeared and I knew I was there to pray for him as well. I woke up hot and sweating still in the midst of praising God & worshiping thinking to myself what just happened. Wow that was amazing God I can't wait till the next time. All I kept thinking was I want to run to church and tell Pastor Portia.

When I finally got to church. I was so excited; I couldn't even tell you what that service was about. I was supposed to be paying attention. That did not happen at all, all I wanted to do was tell her what amazing new thing just happened to me. I waited in line so eager to tell Pastor P after service what happened. I said pastor God has been sending me people to pray for in my dreams. She looked at me so calmly and said, so what did you do? I said, I was obedient and prayed for them. I then said in my vision I can pray so effortlessly and know exactly what to say and how to say it. How do I do that in person? She said it takes practice you just have to do it. To get better at it. I said ok and walked away like wow I really have to do that!

1-7-13

Give God access and watch him transform you!

Early

Up so very early while the world around me is very still

Deep in my thoughts

Or is the creator of my thoughts bringing out the deep in me

For real.

The creator says call on me no matter the hour

Or has he called on me in that hour I'm still.

He moves in me with subtlety,

Subtly changing everything I thought to be,

Thought was me.

Creating new paths

New destinies and a new future for me

Broadening my scope, my view on all that I thought I knew to be.

He has given me a crystal-clear view of me

So, I can see in the compact size mirror he holds

Showing me that part of me he wants me to see

So, I can know just how much he values me

Loves me

He's showing me the areas of my life he wants me to set free

To change

Grow

Learn to live in abundantly

You see

GOD is a gentleman he's not going to show me all of me that needs to be set free

Not all at once, that will be overwhelming for me to see

He wants my life changes to be everlasting

Intentionally

So that I don't return to that person I used to be

He loves me so much it's overwhelming me

The tears are flowing

My mind

My thoughts

My heart

My entire countenance is shifting changing rearranging and growing

As my tears leave my eyes

Roll of my face

And caught by my angels to be taken to thee

I am free

My tears of love are an honor to thee

To me

Of just how he completely loves me

And I love he

So, I say

I'm up so very early

While the world around me is still

Oooh so very deep in my thoughts

Or is the creator of thought bringing out the deep in me

For real

8-1- 2015

Stormcloud Of Anger

A few years back our VCMICC church had an event that the Apostles attended and spoke at. I remember sitting on the left-hand side of the church if you were facing the altar. That particular day I was filled with so much rage and anger that I could not shake it off me, or my thoughts, it consumed me. I knew despite how I was feeling that I needed to be in the church to shift my atmosphere. What I did not know was that despite the smile I whore on my face, my rage had a visible presence that could be seen and noticed by the apostles. I felt a mega storm could looming over me as I sat there trying to forget my issues and pay attention. At one point I felt as if that storm that was brewing and looming above me transformed into a winged dragon over me. I was sitting there like I'm seeing stuff that ain't real.

I know that sounds strange it definitely felt strange to me. To have that be the visions of myself that I was seeing. At that time, I just knew I was tripping and could not at all have really seen that. From the altar I see and hear Apostle Tony say to Apostle Cynthia do you see that? She says yes as they both looked toward the direction in which I was sitting. In my mind, I was thinking I know they not looking over here at me. So, I look from side to side and say oh yes, they are! I look up and say ooohhh wow can they see this on me what the …. I remember wanting so desperately for them to come and lay hands on me. Cast this storm out that I was feeling to make all things new in me and better. I remember being afraid to walk up a be prayed for. So, I just sat there wearing a mask of me, so, I thought! Which was something I did well. I mastered that. Hiding, hiding my pain.

Service was over, the Apostles had to walk past me when they walked down the aisle. I wanted them to look at me, notice me! Notice me screaming with a smile on my face. They just looked straight ahead never once turning my way. I wondered for a while what happened and what I did wrong. Should I have run up to the altar crying pray for me, please! get this off of me. I knew where I needed to be, so I was. I did not know at that time how to be bolder and more intentional in God. I was timid, scared of what others may think of me. Silently wondering, would they be judging me! or was I just judging myself?

Time is your biggest asset that you cannot get back.
Don't waste it in any form!

Mask of Me

I wear a mask of me hiding what I do not want the world to see

If the world could see what I hide so deep down in me they'll scream

Let it free

Let it free

Let it free

Let it free to be

But you see what I want you to see a mask of me

I wear a mask hiding the pain and all the shame that I have that I can't bear to free

Some that was given to me through my lineage and some that I have created in my foolish haste of me

But you see a mask of me you see what I want you to see.

You see what I dare not let the world see what I hide so deep down in me

I hide a world of hurt and pain and strain that I need to let free

But for the life of me can't seem to be free of all the things that ingulf me

How oh how do I dare to be free off the things that plague me when I can't even bare to be free of me.

But I wear a mask of me hiding what I do not want the world to see

If the world could see beneath this mask of me they'll scream

Let it free
Let it free
Let it free
Let it free to be

2010

Prayer & Meditation

A couple of weeks ago maybe three. I went into prayer and meditation on a Friday night feeling really emotional and mad that I was left by someone again for a second time. While in Prayer God took me to a place in heaven I have never been and have no idea what it meant that I was there.

The vision was hazy. I went through a square-long hall or tunnel that had a lit room at the end. I remember the walls feeling hazy and tan-colored. Once I got to the end of the hall to the room. I just stood there looking around. There were people walking back and forth crossing each other with long tan robes. The robes had embroidery going down the front on the sides. Their hair was brown some were black but I could not see their faces. Their faces were all glowing white light. They looked like they were at work. at work looking at documents while walking around. Just as slowly as I seemingly floated and approached the doorway or opening. I was drawn back. I was only there for what seemed like a few seconds.

In prayer, I was asking God what to do about my situation. After being there I heard God say wait. At first, I was like on what God! But now my thinking is I will wait lord, on everything regarding the situation. I gave that situation to God and I stopped worrying about what I could not control. Realizing that giving it to God has always been the best thing. Sometimes waiting and not worrying can seem very hard to do. But that's when faith and trust in the creator have to be at the forefront and you let that lead you and the circumstances.

There is nothing in your life that does not involve God or that you should leave God out of!

Leaps and Bounds

I take leaps and bounds
to understand my purpose and your plan
But I can never seem to understand
Why was I chosen
This is complicated and foreign
Each day that is new
Which is every day of life anew
What I need
I don't get
But the things I want
come to me
what do you do
when all your balls are up in the air
and you can't seem to catch them at all

Disconnected

I had another weird dream for the second time. In this dream, I'm doing stuff for people and saving people. I have no clue who these people are. In the end, it's me and the man I love, we both fall. When I fell, I land, and this big clear spear that has, black and white smaller-sized crystals in it with a big blue center crystal fell from me. When the spear hits the ground some of the black and white crystals fall out and some remain in the spear the big blue crystal comes rolling out as well. In my dream, I am watching myself be distraught and know somehow this is my last chance because it has disconnected before. I instinctively knew I put them back together the first time I fell when I was alone but the time when I fell, I was with my love.

I run over to my man and tell him I guess this is it. He says I thought after how you have changed and everything you have done. I thought they would have let you take it with you. I tell him how much I love him and how he has meant the world to me. In the same breath, I realized that all that I just said to him was not true to my heart. I had a mini flashback of cheating and lying to him but I still confessed my love because I did just love him that much. So, to me it was true. I said goodbye! I love you! You mean the world to me! He was laying on his back wearing a red shirt blue jeans and tan timberlands. I floated up as if I was on an invisible elevator. I watched myself leave him lying there on his back.

On the elevator ride up. I guess I was wondering how true my love really was. If I could have done those things to this person even though I still felt there was true love there between us. When I looked around the floor was all white, with gold or brass rales surrounding it in a circle. I felt such a sense of loss when the spear disconnected from me the second time. I felt like the blue crystal was my soul or my all-seeing eye and the black crystals were the wrong I have done mixed in with the good. I remember putting the blue crystal in the middle making sure to surround it with the mix of other crystals.

During this dream, I watched myself the whole time. I saw my own face looking back at me. I saw my own reactions when I felt or realized that what I was saying did not match what I felt in my heart of hearts. I guess I needed to see what It felt like to lie to myself.

1-5-2009

The real road is looking at yourself with different eyes!

Metaphysical

My metaphysical is fighting my flesh to be with you

My flesh stays out of fear of the unknown

My metaphysical wants to flee, it's being held back by me, or is it thee

Or is it just the entity that incases me

I never know in this life what is wrong and what is right

I can't find the path in life I'm meant to lead or has it found me

I don't know if I'm on it or if it is on me

If I let my spirit free and let it take over me

Will I be able to hang on as it flies me through this life

Taking me to the unknown throughout my life

10-13-10

Unveiled

In my dream, I was lying on the floor in an all-white room naked face down on my stomach before my pastors. My head was turned away from them, they were on my left-hand side. I had a heavy black hallow big pipe or bar across my back holding me down on the floor. The Pastors put their hands on the top of my back to pray for me. I watched myself go back and forth from laying on the floor in this white room feeling the hollow pipe on my back to flying above myself, watching myself go through it. Wondering why in the world am naked before my pastors.

I called My Pastor that next day and told her about the dream she said being naked can mean I'm not hiding anything or I'm revealed or unveiled before them and GOD.

What are the whispers in your life?

Be still and listen to what God is trying to tell you and what directions you need to take in life before you make decision.
Take a moment!

Life Without

Life without _____ is not worth anything

Love

Happiness

Giving

Strength

Faith

Hope

God

12-29-2008

I Thought They Made That Up

When my husband and I started going to Victory about 11 years ago we both went up for prayer together. I grabbed his hand. I remember we were standing to the right-hand side if you were facing the altar. The praise team was singing in the background. This was the first time I remember God showing me his power and control. The pastor where speaking I have no idea what was being said. Everything sound-wise just faded out and went away. I remember standing there and them coming to rolling back and forth on the carpet. I had absolutely no control over my body. I only could see out of my eyes. I remember seeing the pastor holding a microphone and wearing a white shirt. As she jumped over me with the assistance of Pastor D. as I rolled back and forth.

At one point I remember laying on my back with my arms jerking about speaking to God. I do not know what I was saying at all. I came to. Sat up feeling exhausted and a little scared. I sat there for a minute or two to collect myself. I felt like everyone was looking at me. I remember feeling like I wanted to get up and bolt straight out of the room. I just kept darting my eyes back and forth to see if people were actually looking at me and they were. Someone helped me up. scared and trembling, I went back to my seat wanting to go hide so desperately. See, just going to the altar at that time was a super big deal for me, and then to be completely wrecked in the supernatural was otherworldly. I really thought in all my years of going to church that people made that up to show off and show out in church on Sunday.

I asked my husband on the ride home what happened. He looked at me like I was completely crazy! like you did it! why don't you know? I told him what I remembered; he said when I collapsed (which is the last thing I remembered) some men in the church caught me before I hit the floor. I said nobody was touching me what are you talking about? He said they laid me down. I then said to him, I floated to a room in heaven with nothing in it. I was just there but I knew it was where God was and then I was back in my body looking through my eyes like they were just widows too somewhere else. He said I just watched you rolling and jerking there was nothing I could do! I would catch him giving me these strange looks every now and then for the next few days like who is this and what was that?

The following Sunday Pastor Portia said don't forget the powerful move of God that just took place in here last Sunday it was life-changing. I looked around to see if people were looking at me. I do not think they were but I wanted to melt into the floor. She called us into their office I believe a week later I was still very embarrassed even though if anybody understood what happened to me it would be the pastors. I told her that I thought people made that stuff up, which I did! But I was so embarrassed that I really did not want to talk about it. You see, as carefree and free-spirited as I am. I have stage fright; I don't want all eyes on me. It makes me so nervous. God is pushing and growing me.

Seek after the one who first sought after you!

Doesn't Come Easy

Sleep doesn't come easy

When your mind is heavy and your heart is not at ease

Because of all your hopes and dreams

That are halted and stalled

Because you love someone you should not love at all.

When people can't see past their own greed

To plant nurture and water seeds

My angels guide me to see

What I need to see to set me free

To find someone who deserves all that is me

I love too hard and too much to where it seems at times it's a hindrance to me

I pray and wish that it will be given back to me

I love to hard and give too much of me to other entities

But if what I love don't love me

The way I deserve to be

I will set it free

So, I can be loved the way I need and crave to be

So, watch out world when it's time for me to do me

9- 1- 2011

Bound

Lying in bed meditating and singing over and over Tamela Mann's song, take me to the king. I had just prayed and asked god to save me. Which is one of my normal prayers. While in meditation I hear (Renita …….. Stop letting that man keep you bound). The very next thing I see while still meditating is myself walking to the alter holding papers in my left hand that hold all my cares. As I hold up what looked like ripped papers in my hand to leave at the alter GOD takes the papers and they poof disappear. In the natural world, I feel them in my hand disappear like a small explosion. I get up so full and grateful.

What God has for you is not limited by where you are!

I Thought

I thought I had it, meaning my life all figured out

I thought I was on the right path

After a few miles, I looked up and realized the path I took was so wrong and I was so lost.

I thought I went too far to turn back.

I soon realized that there are always detours both good and bad along the way

A few I took thinking they were safe put me back on the original path I was lost on

And others I was damn afraid of the uncertainty of the terrain so I bypassed.

But maybe should have taken thinking the road less traveled was the best

But maybe the more obstacles the better way.

See in life sometimes you have to go through and grow to know!

9-18-2000

We Walk By Faith & Not By Sight

The Monday night following the fear and faith service. I had the most amazing and awesome vision ever. It was of myself and others entering a blue glowing cloud in the sky. I was standing outside of myself watching myself go in between watching myself and being in myself if that makes any sense at all.

I floated up into the sky and floated into a big blue pretty glowing cloud. I entered on the left-hand side right behind me was a man in a wheelchair and behind him, there was this little girl. They were both lit in this blue and white speckled glowing light.

I was looking around wondering what was going on and where I was. I was surrounded by people chanting "We walk by faith and not sight" We are here to spread the love of God. The crowd is repeating this over and over again. Once again, I see myself watching it and going back and forth between watching it and being a part of it at the same time. Meanwhile, people keep entering.

I turn around to see what was behind me. I noticed a huge city in the distance that has big black and dark gray buildings with red and smokey grey everywhere around the buildings. With people who kept changing back and forth between demon faces and human faces, some looked like just demons some looked like people. They were running around everywhere all through the streets in and out of the buildings. I looked to my left and to my right to see if anyone else saw what I was seeing. I noticed the blue and white glowing crowd I was in was growing bigger and bigger and that the cloud was actually people. We were moving and growing and moving and growing. We were moving from city to city in the sky across the world hovering over each city.

As we hovered, I looked to the left and right at each person in the cloud. Each person in the cloud was touching someone in the cities beneath us. We are telling each person we touch that God loves them. Some of the people in the cities are fighting us trying to stop us, and others in the cities that we are touching and telling them that God loves them, are turning into the blue glowing white light, are floating up into the cloud of people with us. As people enter, we grow bigger and bigger and start to move over to other cities, towns, and countries across the world. As I look out, I can see Asian cities, Indian cities, and African cities in the distance.

As I look at the cities in the distance the cities zoom into focus and I can see everything that going on in the cities. We touch people in these cities as we zoom toward them and then hover over them touching people in them. I look back at the people in the cloud where I am they are reciting we walk in faith and not by sight we spread the love of God

4-8-2014

Open yourself to questioning the world around you and everything, "you know" to be in it!

Give Me You

Give me you let me die to my flesh

Please help me put it to rest

So, I can fill myself with the best

I cry out ooh lord for your restful place

Where I am free to just be sin free

Loving in a world that is clear

Where we soar, sing, and live free

Loving you and you loving me

Where there is no pain, strain, or blame

Give Me You!

How To See

During a seeing in the heavenly realm session at church. We were taught and instructed on how to tap into the gifts that God has for us. God showed me something pretty spectacular. We were instructed to close our eyes and hold out our hands. God gave me a dark purple and dark green striped shimmering box with a big full purple bow. I opened the box it was a cloud inside floating, as I seemingly held the cloud in my hands it just kept changing shape for several minutes until it flattened out almost like a sheet of paper.

The paper disappeared and there lay a beautifully ornate golden almost bronze medallion with an amber-colored glass face that you could see straight through. The medallion had a loop at the top that this thick braided leather cord was through. Through the amber glass were words I could not read. I looked the medallion over up and down. I soon noticed that it opened up. I noticed the latch on the side and the seam going around the medallion. I wanted to open it but God didn't let me, I tried to. It felt like it wasn't time for me to open it yet. I wasn't ready. During this whole encounter, there was this warm sweet amber cinnamon smell that kept wisping past my nose

Hebrews 11:1 - Pure in heart

Matthew 5:8 - How do I see? you see by getting to know the holy spirit

John 16:7 - Giving God your imagination

Genesis 11:6 – Why do I need to see? God wants to communicate with you

God wants to open your eyes, for you to live in the supernatural world!

Faith causes you to see in the spirit realm!

My Angels

My Angels guide me to see

What I need to see

They show me the things

You try so hard to hide from me

They protect me

From the things, you don't!

Pastor Gregg Redding

Service in church was powerful and moving. The pastors completely felt the presence of God. Pastor Portia and Pastor Demond asked Elder Bell and his wife to join them at the altar. The pastors were looking at each other like do you feel the presence of the lord it's heavy. Pastor Portia began to pray in tongues so did elder Bell and his wife. I'm looking around like Lord what is going on? I saw at that moment that God was there. He was walking up and down the aisles of the sanctuary. In the sanctuary, I am literally turning my head to face where God is walking around and crying all at once. One of the church members rubs my back and asked me if was I ok. I replied Yes!

Decan Gregg was called to the altar, Pastor Demond said we cannot wait till ordination day we were led by God to do this right now! Decan Gregg looked puzzled. The pastors all began to pray for him. The congregation all stretched out their hands in agreement and prayed as well. Decan Gregg was told to get on his knees at that moment I saw God walk up and stand right behind him with his hand now on Pastor Gregg Redding's Shoulder. God remained there for the duration of the time he was knighted by the elders and prayed for by the Pastors. I remember Elder Bell saying he was called to do great things for the kingdom of God.

After service, Pastor Gregg was overcome with joy. I obeyed God and went up to Pastor Gregg to let him know he was honored and blessed by God. I let Pastor Gregg know exactly what I had witnessed. He told me, thank you so much for your obedience.

Are you what you present?

A Shifting

While sleeping God showed me a shower. I could only see the shower walls. I looked at the wall puzzled as to what it was doing. The wall started warping and I could quite make out what was happening at that moment. And then all of a sudden, the whole wall shifted completely out of place. The tiles were not broken they just completely shifted to the right and down. You could see the pattern that the wall was placed in. it was just not connected anymore.

11-1-2022

You never give your power to those who consider power to be their source of strength!

Heart & Mind

If my heart leads the ways

I'll stay

If my mind tells me so

I'll go

Will they combine

to depict my future fate and destiny

Only time knows where I will grow

When will I ever know

10-21-2010

Over And Over Again

For about 5 or 6 years. God gave me the same dream just in different variations or forms. In these dreams, I am searching for something I just can't seem to find no matter how hard I look. In one of these crazy dreams, I'm getting ready to go out and hang with my girls for a night out on the town. I go to my closet and pick out the perfect flatter all my curves outfit. I go get dressed. I'm singing and dancing in the mirror getting my hair and makeup just right. You know feeling myself and feeling good. My girls come by, knock on the door, and ask me if was I ready. I say, yeah! let me grab my shoes. They go wait for me in the car.

I go into the closet to grab this specific pair of shoes that I know will set this outfit off perfectly. I looked for them where I knew they should have been. I look but can't seem to find them. I'm moving stuff all around. I'm opening every shoe box, tossing shoes behind me, frantically looking for something I know I have and where I left them. Frantically looking because I know my girls are waiting. I see other shoes that will work but those are not good enough. I want the perfect ones that saw in my mind that I know are in there. I cannot stop looking and looking and looking. I'm now sitting in a sea of shoes and boxes and still can't find the ones I want. I then wake up breathing hard, feeling mad and irritated.

In another dream, I went to the mall to buy a pair of jeans. I know the particular store I want to go to and where it is in the mall. I walk through the mall looking at all the store names and lights thinking where is the store? Normally it's right here, as I stand in one spot looking confused. I ask someone walking past if they know where the store is. They say it is just down the way. I walk to where they directed me, never finding the store passing the same stores over and over again walking in circles. Once I woke up, I was like what was that about?

Part two that same dream came months later. I'm back at the mall looking for jeans. (Y'all, I don't like mall shopping at all) This time I walk into the mall and go directly to the store. I'm looking through what's on the display tables. I see the perfect pair. Pick them out excited! Like, yes! these are cute. I go to the dressing rooms to try them on and they don't fit. I ask the attendant to check the size, she gives me another pair and those don't fit either. With each pair I look at myself in the mirror they are all big and baggy. I'm confused and don't understand what's going on. The size is correct, and the cut of the jeans is correct, they just don't fit. I try on pair after pair never finding the pair that fit me perfectly.

Over the years several variations of the same message in my dreams just in different forms just kept coming my way. To the point where I was like look, God, I do not want to have this dream again at all! I'm sick of having these dreams where I'm obviously lost or I'm looking for something and I just can't seem to find it. I don't get it, God! why do I keep having these dreams with no outcome? I noticed just this year, The one thing I never took the time to do with my confusion and frustration over the years with this was to actually ask God what does it mean and what was he trying to show me and teach me. I had even written a poem about looking for something I can't seem to find. But somehow, I never saw the coalition between my vast amount of dreams on this and my poem. Now, I'm like just how dense can I really be? I mean, really! It took me this long to figure this out. For me to get and understand just exactly what God was trying to show me.

I was out here in this big bad world looking for something I was absolutely never meant to find on my own. Bumping into walls with my eyes wide open watching myself hit them over and over. See what I've learned is that God supplies all your needs wants and desires. Every single thing you could ever think of and imagine. God can and will provide. He will make provisions for them to come to you. You need only trust in him and not in your own understanding. Every single time I tried to make things happen on my own it backfired in various ways which lead to hardship, hard work, and hard times. God has already preordained and predestined your life. He is just waiting for you to get in position and in line with it, to receive everything he has for you. Trust in him to lead and guide you through and to your destiny.

When you understand your value in God you move and treat yourself differently!

Looking

I'm looking for something in life I can't seem to find

Peace

Hope

Strength

Freedom

Longing

Affection

Desire

Passion

Romance

Attention

Desperation

Intensity

Touch

Gentleness

Kisses

Hugs

I'm looking! I'm looking! I'm looking! I'm looking

For

True Love

4-4-2008

Cyclone

During Bible study, God gave me a vision of myself. We were instructed during service to raise our hands high. I raised my hands God showed me my hands held high there was fragmented black muck moving slowly and completely surrounding me from head to toe as if I was standing in the middle of a cyclone. When my hand touched the muck, it was sticky like tar would be. I remember in the natural I pulled my hand down looking at it like what is this?

In the supernatural in slow motion, I pulled my hand back from it and it slowly pulled away from my finger going back into the cyclone to continue moving around me slowly. I remember feeling like it was going to consume me. I went up for prayer that following Sunday. I explained in detail to the pastor what I had seen. She said let me pray for you. I said yes very eagerly. I did not want to be consumed by whatever that was.

Your thoughts create and shape your reality!

Left Alone

I hate to be left alone in my head

So, I watch TV instead

Drowning myself in someone else's fictional sense of reality or is it real TV

Their lives lived my life cried feeling always as if on the verge and never knowing why

Wondering why I can't set myself free to be

I'm keeping myself bound by not first loving thee

But spending too much attention loving a man who I thought loved me.

12-8-2012

Spiritual Retreat

Last night I had the most amazing dream/ revelation/ spiritual encounter with Apostle Tony. I believe I was at a spiritual retreat. It started with me waking up in a room in my pajamas. I was on a bed with a big picture bay window. That was at the foot of the bed. as I looked out of the window there were tall trees and a pretty blue sky. The room was very calm in feel and sight with cool shades of cream and tans with pops of burgundy and cranberry colors everywhere. Pastor Tony came into the room and sat in a chair that was on the left-hand side of the room. I was sitting on the bed. We talked about me and my life what seemed like for hours. At the end of the conversation, he told me to make sure I keep the cat out of the room. I said okay. There were other women in the house that came to my room. I said to them to hurry and make sure the cat doesn't get in. As they were opening the door that cat ran in and sat on the bed and looked me directly in the face. I said ooh no he can't be in here. So, I put him out. The ladies and I talked for a while. As we were beginning to leave the room the cat flew up the stairway and tried to get back into the room again. I held him back with my foot as I closed the door he nipped at my heels as if he was mad and tried to bite me.

I closed the door until I heard it click. I noticed across the hallway floor there was a pile of keys each set belonging to one of us ladies. One of the ladies said Renita I need your keys I left something in the car. I said okay and looked at the pile. I saw what I thought looked like my keys and said those aren't mine. mine is in my purse in my room. I knew they weren't mine because mine had a red house key chain that was brand new. The keys that were on the floor had the same red house key chain but you could tell it was an old house on the key chain it was faded and worn. The girl who called my name proceeded to go get the keys out of my purse in my room. The cat flew up the stairwell again trying to get in the room we all held him back. She got the keys came out of the room and quickly shut the door. I looked back because I wasn't sure if I heard the door make that click letting me know it was shut tight.

We all went down the stairs and outside to the end of the driveway where Apostle Tony stood next to some very tall hedges that blocked the view of the house from where we were. Apostle Tony began to tell us about how he had to tie the dog and cat to the back of his car bumper and drag them down the street to get rid of them. I am assuming this was metaphorically speaking of course. We went back inside the house to our rooms for a while. I remember sitting and meditating back in my room. I put on my blue comfy robe and then went back down the stairs to meet Apostle Tony in the kitchen. I passed a lady who was on my left, who spoke to me. I can't remember what we spoke about but we had a deep meaningful conversation.

I proceeded to the kitchen where there was someone whom I somehow knew who was sitting to my left. I asked her where was grandma, she told me she is taking a nap. There was another lady standing behind the kitchen island who was mixing food in a bowl. I walked over to Apostle Tony who was sitting at the island. He asked me something I do not quite remember, but I remembered my response. I said I don't have a mom and dad who can help me financially. I have to depend on myself. As I was saying that I looked at the lady who was cooking she looked up at me slightly and continued cooking. Apostle Tony then said as he held my hand "you have the grace to do everything you need to do just like that Bomb, Bomb, Bomb as my hand went downward with each Bomb" to me meaning it will all fall in line step by step. This encounter filled my whole entire night. The black cat would run or zoom by so fast it would almost look like smoke. I remember thinking this once I woke up.

The way you do anything is how you do everything!
Read That Again, and now Read It Again!

Awake

I awake to the world with simple notes of affirmation and praise.

To the joy of the thought, I've put in someone else's days.

I am made over a new each day

I feel like silk, raw and simplistic to its origin and existence,

knowing I'm destined to be handled and cherished with care

you are as gentle as cashmere to the touch of life and love

which I am drawn to like a moth to a flame

you inspire me to be

to be

to be

to be

loved, engulfed, indulged, quenched, drenched, submerged, and devoured

by all things that bring a smile to my world

with you the mere fragments of the formulation of thought are sweet

you make me understand that I am deserving of appraisal and adoration to my existence.

9-11-2009

Invisible Friend

As a child, I had a friend in the spirit realm that no one saw but me. Now, I don't remember this at all! I do remember my mother telling me these stories periodically throughout my life. My mom would say as a child you had an imaginary friend, whom I had to prepare a plate of food for when I made yours. She would tell me that I would demand that she make him a plate of food. She said that she would just so that I would eat because if she didn't, I would be sad and wouldn't eat my food. I said mom, I don't remember this, none of that, at all! She said yes, it's true.

My mom told me I would tell her or others don't sit there David is sitting there. She said she would catch me running through the house and she would ask what are you doing. My response would be, me and David are playing tag. She said she would leave me be and let me play. I asked her how old was I when this started, and she said about 2 and it lasted till I was almost 4. She said once David left, loneliness or sadness came over me and I did not want to be involved with other kids. I was content playing alone. I have always been a loner kind of kid and person. I have always marched to the beat of my own drum. Never cared much about what other kids were into or why. I have always been happy in my own world!

Nothing and no one, has no rights to determine you and your outcome!

Anticipation

God knew I was troubled and toiling with a lot. I needed to know what to do and how to do it. I was wondering why this and why that on so many things. I was looking at this beautiful orange leather purse for a while that I wanted to purchase for myself as a birthday gift. When I went to go purchase it was completely sold out. I had waited too long to get the bag. So, I had to make another choice or move on. I noticed that they had the same bag in white, white canvas with black leather trim and black details that I decided I liked. My brother asked me what did I want for my birthday I sent him a picture of the bag. He ordered the bag and had it shipped to me. I'm over elated and so excited.

The dream picks up with me waiting for this bag to arrive. In the dream, I had to go online again and pick another option just like I had to do in real life. The option that I picked this time was the same style bag only this one had different color paint all on the white canvas bag. I was so excited checking the mail every day waiting eagerly for my package. It finally came I open the box with the biggest smile on my face. I pull it out it is not what I chose at all. What I received after much anticipation was a clear plastic purse with patches of painted-on colors. I went back and forth with can I return this or do I just have to deal with it and work with it. Which is what I would tend to do, make the best out of a bad situation. As I looked at the bag with more detail trying to decide if I could use it. I noticed hole, after hole, after hole all along the bottom. As I am touching it my fingers are going straight through the holes.

God reminded me of this vision that I had completely forgotten about that I had just had hours ago. I had so much I was toiling with on my mind that I did not get up and write it down. He gave it back to me on my drive to work that morning. My daily talk with God is God use me. How can I be of use to you today? What do you want me to do today? That's when he reminded me of what he showed me. God showed me that What YOU ordered and anticipated is not what you received or got. You received a clear plastic painted-on bag with holes in the bottom. I don't have to keep something and try to make something work. I can return it to the sender. I deserve so much more than a clear plastic-painted on bag, with holes in it! He showed me that I tried to make something work that I was never meant to have. It was painted on with holes in its foundation which means it could not hold anything. The painted outer walls were all a façade of the trouble that loomed beneath.

11-7-2022

Sometimes we as people hold onto things and people so tightly that God is trying to tell us to let go of. Because of fear we hold on, knowing God is saying throw up your hands and let it all go!

When Life Is Life-ing

When life is life-ing real hard, you need to turn to the word of God

to pull you through, guide you through, completely stop you from being a fool.

When life is life-ing real hard, he is there to stop you from running up,

stop you from jumping up, stop you from cutting up, stop you running amuck.

When life is life-ing real hard, drop to your knees and praise God

for keeping you sane when all you want to do is completely raise Kaine.

When life is life-ing real hard, open your bible and pick out any bar

to stand on and shout about, not run to one trying to figure it out.

When life is life-ing real hard, remember whose you are,

remember who shaped you, molded you, remember it's he that holds you.

When life is life-ing real hard, do you stand or do you fall, who do you call

do you turn to God, he knows the purpose and the plan of it all.

When life is life-ing real hard, all you need to do is just turn to God!

11-6-2022

Mommy & McDonald's

God is always speaking are you listening?

My mom and I were hanging out and spending the day running small errands. We decided to go inside the McDonald's to sit and take our time to eat. We got our food set by a big bay window that this particular McDonald's had. To my left sat a police officer facing me that was maybe a row back from where we were sitting my mom sat with her back toward the officer and to the left of me. My mom and I were just talking. That kind of talking where you are jumping in and out of different subjects and topics just enjoying each other company.

At one point in the conversation, while my mom was talking, I heard God say Renita. I looked up. Simultaneously while I'm listening to God, I can see the officer and my mom both looking at me like what is happening. I can see my mom looking out the corner of her eye at me while eating her french fries real slow. The officer is looking at me while sipping his soda. I say yes! God says. Tell your mom I am waiting for her. I say yes sir. I look at my mom and say Mommy God just told me to tell you that he is waiting for you.

She looks at me and her eyes start to fill with tears. I asked her what was wrong. My mom told me that she was afraid to give herself completely to God because she might die once she does. I asked my mom why do you think that. She said it's because of the life I have led! I think once I give myself to God, he is going to call me home. I said mom God got you and he is going to take care of you he loves you mommy trust him.

You are not defined by your past you are prepared by your past!

Heart

I have a very good heart,

Sometimes it's hard to find

Buried beneath the mountain of things,

That plague my mind

You see,

I'm learning how to let things go

Leave them to the one,

The only one who knows where they go

You see,

I was not built and meant to carry such cares

That's why

I ache and sigh and cry

Because they need to be released

 And given to thee

So, I can live free

The God Of Cars & Your Safety

For a few weeks, I kept praying and talking to God. Asking him and telling him I wanted and needed a car badly. The one I had leaked gas so bad you could smell it. I was literally driving around in a bomb. I searched around and asked friends where was the best place to go. One of my friends told me to go to eastern motors. I called and set the appointment up for a couple of weeks later when I knew I would have more money, so, I could put a nice down payment down. I thought to myself ok it's settled this is what I'm doing, I'm going to eastern motors. God woke me up early that next Saturday morning and said go get a car. Loud and clear as day. I didn't think twice. I immediately got up jumped in the shower got dressed and ran out of the house.

Got in my gas-leaking hooptie and started on my way to eastern motors. Eastern motors was an Hour and a half from where I lived. I got maybe 15min from my door and my car cut off for the first time while I was driving, I had no time to even pull over. Luckily for me, there weren't many cars on the road. I immediately restarted my car and restarted my journey ten minutes later my car stopped again when I stopped at a red light. I said OK that's it I'm going home. I made a U-turn and started back toward my house. I heard God speak again he said turn around and go get a car. I said okay and turned back around my car did not break down again.

I called my aunt and asked her to ride with me because I had absolutely no clue about what to do or how to haggle when purchasing a car. I picked my aunt up. She asked where I wanted to go, I told her eastern motors. She said No you definitely don't want to go there. Let's try Carmax the closes one was in Laurel MD which was almost an hour from where she was. We get to Carmax without the car breaking down again. I had absolutely no credit and only $500 to purchase a car. I treaded my hooptie in for $250 I walked away with a Kia Rondo with a V6 engine which was a stick and an automatic that only had 50,000 miles on it. I was very grateful and happy that I listen to God, He literally cares about you and your heart's desires.

I woke up on that very next Sunday morning with fear thinking about what just happened and what did I do. Did I make a good decision? Did I make the right choice in cars? See the devil knows that one of my weaknesses and biggest fears are making the wrong choices in life. Scared to step out of fear of not being good enough or failing.

During church in praise and worship, I had to come to myself and realize the blessing that was just given to me and whom it came from. When all the odds looked or seemed like they were against me my God delivered.

I stepped out on his words and in faith

I will not operate in fear

1st John 5:4.

The love of God will give you total deliverance of any and everything

Come as you are to God's love

His love never fails

The love of God is what changes a man to change and repent, not judging them.

3-10-2013

God can/will bring you what you desire but you must be in place/ position to receive it!

Your Praise

Your praise is the praise I breakthrough

Your praise is the praise I grow through

Your praise is the praise I worship to,

I know through,

I love through,

Give through,

Flow through

Your praise is that place I cry to be

Die to self to be

Your praise is the place I strive to be

Your praise is that place I shine through

Your praise is my free space free place to stay

I worship you lord

It's an honor to be next to thee, loving thee as you love me

Sun Rays

God showed me the sun shining bright in the sky. Everybody in the sanctuary had their hands lifted high, in full worship praising God speaking in tongues and shouting high to the heavens. The sun rays were shooting down from the sun slicing through the people. As the rays sliced through the people, they fell out in the spirit one by one, till half the congregation was slain in the spirit laying on the floor. I was sitting in my seat praising and thanking God taking in what he was showing me.

I then saw the most beautiful intricate wind swirls beautiful mosaic shades of dark blues with white swirls, swirling past my face coming from the left-hand side. I heard cries and with each cry more swirls. I looked to see where and from whom they were coming from. It was Amanda, on the floor slain in the spirit crying out loud. God showed me that her cries were a mosaic van Gough-ish style moving virtual painting of the wind blowing through the congregation with each breath and cry she took.

Access his grace!

Rainbow

I love to watch the rainbows of life

dance across the horizon

as the wind blows past me

and takes my essence to the clouds

as it lies suspended

to rain down on the world

and share my love

11-29-2010

Ordination

God allowed me to witness the Deacon and Minister ordination. He allowed me to see all of heaven cheering and shouting jumping up and down for joy while angles flew in glee above us. All the clouds were shaped like a football stadium it was packed as if it was super bowl Sunday. When I saw how all of heaven rejoices for us. it moved me so much that I could not stop the tears of joy from just flowing down my face. As each person was called up the stadium erupted one after the other, they cheered even harder for the ordained minister and I just cried more and more. I remember one of the church members Tamela touching and rubbing my shoulder asking me if I was ok, while I'm looking up into the heavens just crying.

Do not be conformed to this world, be transformed by the word of God!

Pandemic

I dreamt I was sitting in the very back of the sanctuary near the sound stage. A step dance team entered the sanctuary from the right-hand side if you were facing the stage. The performance was being performed by many different people from the church men, women, boys, girls, and teens. All dancing in the same patterned shoes no matter the style of shoes. Their shoes were all white with black moving snakeskin prints. Some had on sneakers other loafers, some had on dress shoes. One woman I noticed had on knee-high boots. I saw little feet, big feet of all kinds and sizes dancing in unison. During the dance, they were stomping their feet on the floor very hard and aggressively, vibrating and shaking the floor with each step. All of a sudden, they all kicked or took off their shoes and started banging them on the floor with so much force and intensity you could see it on all of their faces.

At that exact same time, I realized that I was using the bathroom in the back of the sanctuary taking a number 2 of all things. It was so much pop I just kept wiping and wiping myself it took a while for it to stop. During the time I was wiping the dancers had left. Pastor D. started preaching. He walked down the left aisle if you are sitting in the back of the church. He came all the way to the back where I was sitting, he never stopped preaching but he kept looking at me with this look like I can't believe this and why aren't you done yet. He walked back and forth a few times giving me this same look each time while still preaching. I was done, I adjusted my clothes and went to go wash my hands which were also in the sanctuary. The whole time I still heard the pastor preaching. There were people sitting behind me the whole time. I noticed them while I was washing my hands over and over again, I was making sure they were clean.

As I finished washing my hands. I noticed Elder Tracey coming in my direction. She came to me twirling in circles and almost dancing with this big floor-length flowy African print skirt that had big patterns and bright colors a white shirt and a head wrap that matched the skirt. She was waving this really long incense as she moved toward me. You could see the smoke trails in the hair that seemed to swirl all around her. When she reached me, she said we are all so glad you are done we could not wait! She lifted the incense in front of me and blew it in my face. I was instantly surrounded by a fragrant cloud of smoke. As the smoke began to dissipate, I looked out and saw Elder Tracey dancing and twirling back to the front of the church to her seat.

I went back to my seat and sat down. I was then asked if I had gotten the letter, I said no! what letter? The lady next to me said the letter regarding the structure and changes to how everything would be run from now on. I said wow more changes. Someone got up to go get me a copy of the letter I grabbed it and then woke up.

I remember thinking what in the world was that? when I woke up. This vision came to me about 2 years before the pandemic. As time went on throughout the pandemic different aspects of the vision became clear, and made sense at different times. God would bring parts to my remembrance of what he showed me. The snakeskin pattern on the shoes was DNA strands that seemed to move. This to me symbolized the different variants of Covid19 strands. The boot-stomping was directly in coalition with finding a vaccine to eradicate the virus to keep people from dying! Hand washing was cleaning your hands by way of sanitizer or soap and water frequently to keep from spreading germs. The part about Pastor D. waiting for me to be done relates to me stepping in place and in line when it comes to church and what God is calling on me to do. Sitting in the back of the church was the social distancing part everyone in the sanctuary was spaced apart. The letter symbolizes how the world will be completely changed and how we will communicate with each other from now on. As you can see there are still parts yet to be revealed. In due time God will unveil what he wants me to know and understand next.

Will you allow fear to move you or will you operate in faith!

Fear

I'm still walking in fear blended with tears

I need to be free of not knowing what maybe or what is for me

Free to see what you want me to see and not what I see that's hiding so deep down in me

My Fear

My Tears

My Blame

My Shame

And way too much Pain

Take them from me

So, I can see

So, I can see

So, I can see

Be free to just be

Loving you as you have always loved me

Even when I did not notice you noticing me

Shining your light oh so bright on me

With all the tears I cried looking for that love that was always there waiting for me

to be free

to accept thee

into me

Now I know with thee

I am free

To be all that you called of me to be

Loving you as you have first loved me

3-11-2012

My Sister

My sweet baby sister Jessika went back home to heaven at 4 months old. That did not stop her from visiting her new baby nephew from heaven. When my son was about 4 months old. We laid down on the bed to take a nap. Y'all know how we moms do, we nap when the baby naps. I put my baby in the middle of the bed and surrounded him with rolled-up blankets and or pillows. I lay beside him sleeping away when I heard the most angelic sound, my baby, making high pitch squeals, cracking up laughing, and kicking his feet at over the place having a good time. I try to wake up to check on my baby but I cannot move my body, it's like I'm frozen in time. At this point, I'm struggling within myself to free myself.

I hear a voice above my head as if she was sitting on the bed at my headboard. The voice says NO! Ree! I came to see the baby. I instinctively knew who it was. The voice belonged to my sister. She sounded like a child. I can hear her. so, I spoke to her. Scared, within myself. I feel myself panicking because I can't move to check on my baby. I say Jessika you need to go back where you came from! She says, Ree! I just want to see the baby please No. I lay there still unable to move. I'm now trying to turn my head toward my baby, I still can't move. Marcus laughs and kicks again happy as he wants to be. I knew she wasn't here to hurt him; he was so happy. I could feel it and hear it. I'm a first-time new mom. so, I'm freaking out on the inside because I can't check on my baby. I can't open my eyes. I can't move only hear and speak! I say Jessika you have to go! I felt her get off the bed. I felt her standing right beside me.

And then she was gone. I could move again. I jumped up grabbed my baby held him and rocked back and forth, crying for such a long time. I told my sister over and over again that I was so very sorry for sending her away. My fear completely got the best of me. Once I got myself together. I called my mother to tell her everything. As I began to explain I started to cry all over again. The act of telling my mother that the baby that preceded her to heaven came to visit her nephew was overwhelming to us both. But such a blessing at the same time. At that time in my life, I did not know or understand how to embrace this tremendous calling and gift that God has placed on my life. It terrified me. I kept the circle very tight of those who knew and my mom was definitely my safe haven. She understood my gift!

I remember when I was about seventeen or eighteen maybe 6months to a year after my sister went to heaven. I would wake up late at night to see my brother who was about 3 almost 4 sitting on the couch or pushing the buttons on the TV until he found the cartoon channel, he would be watching cartoons and laughing holding Jessika's blanket. I would say what are you doing he would say, me and Jessi are watching TV see, as he looked next to him. The very first time this happened I went immediately to my mom's room which was also on the first floor she said, Ree in a very calm tone! He is fine! I got him! You can go back to bed, I gave her this look like, are you sure? She said again calmly, he is okay! He is playing with his sister. She understood us and our gifts! I went back to my room. You know I could not sleep after that! I was just up thinking, I need to go get my baby (my brother) and bring him up here with me. So, I waited until he fell asleep on the couch. I went and got him and put him in the bed with me. I am pretty sure my mom knew I was going to do that.

The two most important days in your life are the day you were born and the day when you discovered why!
What is your gift in life?

Honey

You are as angelic and simplistically complex as your existence.

You are so fresh, breath taken and sweet in your origin.

You drip from your hive enticing the world to dare you, to try you, to want you, to need you, to crave you.

You are nectar in its purest essence. Food from the highest of the high, to the deserving or lucky enough to notice you high in the trees of life.

You are protected by a life force that is strong but easy to cross, angelic in its own right like what it protects.

The sun has kissed you high in the trees and stained you for the world to see in awww of your simplistic beauty and gifts you were given.

You bring a smile to the most fruitful but barren of places.

You are a life-sustaining force to be wrecked with. There is no other on earth who can give what you have.

The formula it took to make you is vast and complex, your secret will never be told.

In time your complexity spills out to be shared by a lucky few who notice you high in the trees.

9-1-2009

In Heaven With My Daughter

I was doing a study on this lady named Kat Kerr and how she sees in the heavenly realm. Just listening to a lot of the things that she has on YouTube. One of her videos is on how your babies in heaven are waiting for you to get there so you can raise them and love on them. Meditating on this really had my heart and soul full.

God allowed me to go to heaven and spend the day with my daughter. I was not ready to have a child at 20. I was still in college living with my boyfriend whom I had no business living with thinking I'm grown. My Naive relationship was not stable, it was just a mess. 22years later God took me on a journey to heaven to see my daughter she was about 5 or 6 years old. she walked right up to me instinctively I knew she is mine. She says mommy what are you doing here. You are not supposed to be here yet. I hugged her. we walked and talked I watched her play. She showed me around. It felt like I was there with her for hours. I remember watching the sunset in heaven. She is the cutest Lil redbone child pretty round face with long red-brown colored hair looking just like her dad and older sister.

I woke up set up in bed and cried the hardest cry. Just sat there rocking myself back and forth. They were tears of so many mixed emotions. I felt joyful that I got to see her and hold her I felt worthy and grateful from and to God that he allowed me to have that moment. I felt so blessed and loved that I knew her and she knew me and called me mommy! My heart is so full and the tears are just flowing remembering that moment as I am typing this. I could barely keep myself together. After I collected myself that day, I immediately called her father and told him of my visit with our daughter. I prayed that he would have the same experience. I also called my mom and cried some more. See this is the first time I actually went to heaven to visit a loved one. I have had several visitations from my loved ones in the past, which I cherish every single moment of.

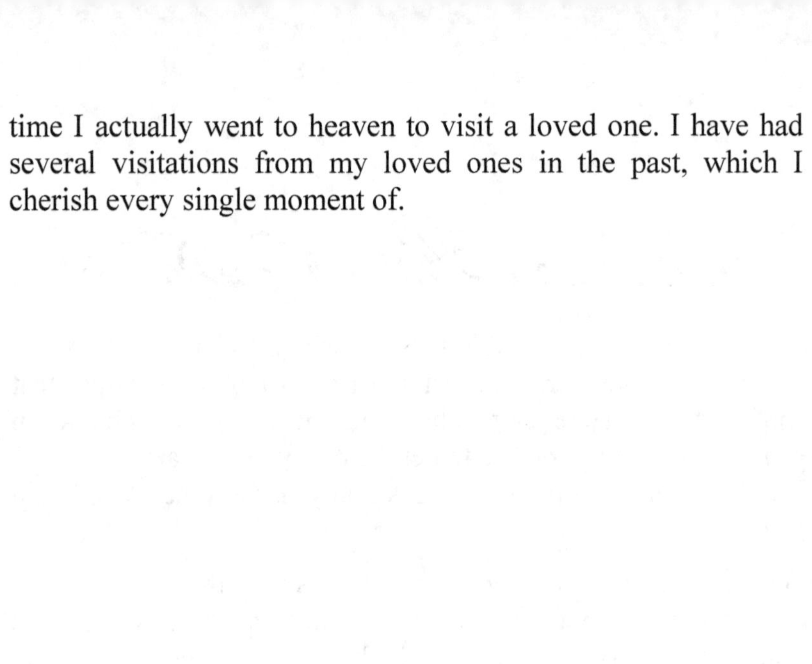

We often block our own blessings because we don't feel worthy enough, you are because you are here!

Reality Or Dream

Sometimes I get lost in your reality or is it really mine

where dragons and unicorns roam free.

And rainbows are endless slides across time

Is there a portal where we touch and life becomes yours and yours becomes mine

Sometimes I can swear that your future, fate, destiny, and time are all mine.

Your life seems so much more interesting than mine.

Skipping through portals defying gravity not obeying time,

rewinding it slowing it down a bit,

manipulating the fabric, the very essence of it.

Your world is free, endless, vibrant, and scary

Layered and intertwined to people, places thought lost to mine

I get lost there not wanting to return to my own

Yours is the place where coma patients lie

not realizing they're lost in a trap of endless bliss and time

To awake to a world where life is fragile and sweet

and has moved on without you in their ultimate defeat

Your world is such an intoxicatingly sweet state to behold

it feels like minutes or even seconds but truly are hours

How do you suspend the most precious thing we own

manipulating it, making it your own

Is your reality home and my world the dream

And yours the true world I wish for in my dreams

Where everything seems to be all right

And problems fade away as the night

While morning brings a new light

10-3-2010

The Fly Old Lady

This lady with a big house and a garden full of fresh produce and brand-name clothes.

This little old lady tended to her garden daily she was always flawless and fly with beautiful long silvery gray hair down her back. On this particular day, she wore a wide-brim hat with a beautiful flowing light blue dress and a beautiful scarf tied around her neck. She always wore new outfits, new hats, purses, and new scarves she made sure to always look good. She hummed and sang as she watered her garden always smiling and happy. The garden was so full seeming as if it was overgrown, it was just bursting with life, just full and luscious. You could see the lady's backyard and house from the street. There was a long stretch of grass that slopped downward to her property with a bench at the midway point that faced her backyard.

The lady died in her house in her bed. Her family just put her treasures out for anyone and everyone to grab. My aunts and family told me about what was going on at the house. So, we all decided to drive by the house. We parked the car at the top of the hill behind her house we could see that everybody there was just grabbing and taking the stuff off the racks as it was a final call sale. The family just kept putting out more stuff just as fast as it was flying out of there. I looked at my aunts and said I am going down to get some stuff too. My family was afraid to go with me. I made my way down and through the crowd of people reaching and grabbing everything in sight. I began grabbing purse after purse, nick knacks, hat after hat, shirts, and scarves. Rushing and moving fast looking through rack after rack grabbing stuff till my arms shoulders and back were full from the bags of stuff I grabbed. I saw an empty bag laying on the floor and began to fill that as well with my new treasures.

I went back to get more, and this time I walked throughout her house knowing I was not supposed to be in there. I walked down the hall peeking into the rooms. inside the house was dark in feeling and in color. I noticed she was still laying in her bed with a smile on her face. She died under her covers. You could smell that her body was starting to rot. Others began to notice the smell and were covering their noises. It was strange you could smell her till you got close to the room. Everyone including myself still looked through her things. As I am coming out of the house, I see my friend Sparkle looking through stuff I tell her that there are a lot of things over there she would like as I pointed behind me. We both began to see all kinds of beautiful treasures from the lady. We were showing them to each other. Like, look what I have found. Girl, you see what I got, back and forth with each other. We are looking all on the shelves in the house grabbing nick knacks off shelves, taking stuff out of her draws all kinds of fancy things that were tucked away out of site.

As we were leaving the house, we saw can goods, baby food bottles, and bottles of juice. I grabbed a box and began to fill it with all this food. Nobody wanted the food but me. They were looking at me like why are you getting all of that when you can get all of this, pointing at her other treasures in the house. I told everyone that the food was in the packaging and still preserved so it is good, take it. I had grabbed so much that I was struggling to carry it all by myself back to the car where my aunts were waiting for me. Everything that I had collected was so much and so heavy that I had to stop at the bench that was just up the hill heading back to ward the street from the back of the ladies' house. I noticed someone tried to bury one of my bags in the dirt. I heard my friend say did you intend to carry that one too as she pointed to the bag partially buried with my items halfway sticking out of the ground. I went to go pull it all up, there was so much stuff buried that when I tried to pull the bag up it broke. I found more empty bags and put all of my things that were buried in them.

I looked up for my ride and hollered for my aunts whom I thought were going to be still waiting for me. They saw all my stuff hopped back in the ride and drove off leaving me hollering for them to come help me. I see my friend and say can you give me a ride. She says I parked over there pointing across a field past a gated basketball court. She says we have to walk. I carried all of my bags of new treasures, a big box of food on my right shoulder all alone. I had so much stuff to carry that it seemed like that long walk would break me and that the bags would break. I struggled with each step and kept readjusting my stuff to get a better grip but kept moving and going. The more I walked on, the bags and the box began to feel effortless and light to carry in all of their abundance. The friend that I am walking with is soon gone and there is someone new I have never seen before walking with me. She is telling me about this big sale that is happening and how everything is so cheap. She says it won't cost you if you have the right coupon or access codes to the abundance. She begins to tell me about this one pair of shoes that were easy to slip into, she says all you have to do is just velcro fasten the top and keep stepping. As she describes them, she said laughingly I don't know who would want them they are for people who eat carrots and veggies all-day kind of shoes. I said think I love carrots and veggies. I want to know what they look like so I can see for myself if I want them. Meanwhile, during all of this, she is telling me how and what to do to get the cheap accessible shoes.

We are still walking, my bags become so light that I no longer noticed them or that I was still carrying them. It was completely effortless carrying my treasures. I looked to see where they were. They are all still with me. I looked again and noticed my hands were in front of me carrying all of my items. They are small everything is still with me just smaller and lighter they fit in the palm of my hands. They were still full bursting at the seams just in the palm of my hands. I continued to carry them all as we smiled, laughed, walked, and talked. I kept looking at her with so much intensity she was so young and vibrant so full of energy, and beautiful. I notice the entire time we are walking her demeanor and presence is fairy-like just carefree and happy. We walked and talked more I kept looking at her like I knew her, she looked and seem so very familiar.

I woke up grabbed my journal and began to write all this down. As I got to the end. I realized that this vibrant beautiful energized young lady walking and talking with me about shopping and shoes was the little old lady with everything renewed and rebirthed in her life. I started to cry in complete awe like God wow you are so amazing. There are so many nuggets to grab out of this! Thank you, God!

Whatever you turn your attention or focus to that is what you will become!

I Am There

Do you know who I am

Do you know where I come from

Do you know where you come from

I am the very essence of who you are

We are

I am

I leave my sweet essence where ever I go

It glides throughout time for this world the next, your future, and mine

We will always be connected by several entities for all time and eternity

Have you ever walked through a bright beam of heavenly warm sunlight

It's an angelic state to behold

Have you seen the very essence of me waiting in that beam of light

Suspended throughout time waiting to meet your acquaintance

As you inhale throughout your life you take me into your soul.

My signature transcends it, it is to be consumed.

That to me is your ultimate doom

Do you feel me as I blow past you?

Dou taste me as you part your lips

You may not feel me or taste me as I come into you but I am there
I left my mark on your essence
I am there.

11-29-2010

Birthday Boots

For a few years, I was on the hunt for a pair of thigh-high boots made for a plus-size woman such as myself. In every store, I went to nothing. And in the many online stores, I would frequently buy boots only to give them away. I would look at the measurements and then dig through the junk draw as if I was looking for gold searching for the measuring tape to see if I measured up to the size, they offered sometimes to buy them anyway hoping there was enough stretch. While online I see the perfect pair of thigh-high brown boots made just for plus sizes. This would be the perfect Birthday present to get me for my 40th. I discovered that they have this wonderful new invention called quad pay. I'm over-elated that I get to break this hefty bill down into four payments. What! say less, I'm like Yes! sign me up.

I purchase the boots and pay the first installment. A week later my boots arrived. I jumped into these boots with quickness and almost fell in my room trying to get them on so fast. Singing and dancing. I'm waving my hands in the air pointing like I'm hyping up a crowd ain't nobody even in the darn house but me and Jesus. Aaaaeee I got my birthday boots, I got MF birthday boots, look at my birthday boots! Aaaeee, Aaaeee, Aaaaeee! I got my birthday boots. Over and over! I was so darn excited I filmed myself singing this song and posted it on FB showing nothing but my boots in the video. Lol! don't judge me I'm still a work in progress.

The following week it was time to pay the second payment. I went to the app, and open it, it says my boots were paid in full and my first payment was sent back. Wait, WHAT! How though! I'm starting to panic thinking, what did I do wrong what happened they gonna come for me. it's gonna be on my credit report. So I calm myself and say ok my first installment was sent back go check your account, it was there, I never noticed it in my account. I then called the company I got my shoes from and said can you check my order #. The representative said your order is paid in full she then said is something wrong I said no and thank you. I hurried up and got off the phone. At that moment I remembered Pastor Portia's sermon on supernatural debt cancellation and how God can move and do things beyond whatever you could think or imagine. I called my brother and said I think God just brought me some boots for my birthday. He said What! and then Aaaaaeeeee, look at God. I said I know! With the most childish happy voice. I got MF birthday boots and I turned up all over again about my boots.

I had forgotten to write this down. God reminded me on the Sunday after the VWCI 2022 after church that day on the drive home that he gave me boots for my 40th Birthday. God most definitely delights in the desires of your heart. It is such an honor to receive a birthday present from the most high. To know that you love me so much to bless me! Is so overwhelming and sweet. Thank you, Father!

Put yourself in a positive state of expectancy!

Love

It is the most beautiful thing in the world

If you are lucky enough to find that very special one in your heart,

the one that you know you will never part

I and He

He and Me

The way true love is supposed to be!

1-24-2010

God Hears Your Desires

About 4 years ago I had a coworker whose significant other sent her flowers every single week. I would call her to the front desk to pick up her flowers. She would have the biggest smile on her face every single time, you could feel the love she felt from him, it was infectious and beautiful to witness. I was like who is this dude, he needs to be cloned. I slapped my hand on the desk and said girl, where did you find him at! He got a brother! Cousin! Uncle! Nephew! Friend! Where God making them at! I need to go there. We all just laughed. It was funny but I lowkey was so serious. I have never received flowers or a gift from my man or any man at work. I have always longed for someone to love me and think of me that much. I yearn to be someone's thought. To feel special and truly loved.

While sitting at the front desk of my Job this lady comes in with this beautiful silver bracelet on each link on the bracelet is a rose. I'm noticing her jewelry while addressing her concerns about what she came into the agency for. I tell her how beautiful the bracelet is. And that I love roses. I showed her the rose tattoos, that I have on both my arm and my wrist. We finish up her paperwork. I said if you don't mind where did she find the bracelet, she took the bracelet off and handed it to me. I said ma'am I can't take your bracelet. She said no I want you to have it. I immediately start to cry and said thank you oh my God thank you so much. I said ma'am can I hug you; she says yes. I am completely sobbing at this point. I ran around the counter like a child at Christmas running to the Christmas tree. I gave her the biggest hug. I told her, thank you probably three or four more times. It took me some time to get myself together after that. I put it on that very second. Word traveled fast through the office that a lady took her bracelet off and handed it to me. My coworkers came up to me for the rest of the day asking me did someone give you a bracelet. I said yes with the biggest smile on my face and stuck my arm out for each of them to look at it. So proud and excited.

 That very night about 3 am God said to me while I was sleeping. Renita, I gave you flowers at work that you can keep. I woke up and sat straight up out of the bed, grabbed my wrist where the bracelet lay and I cried in gratefulness feeling honored, loved, and tremendously blessed that he loved me so much that he took the time to give me my heart's desire flowers at work! I will forever be amazed every single time at God's love for me. I get so excited and feel so full of love.

You are a mirror reflection of God and who he is!

Just Me

I breathe and exist in realms, which you dare not see

When I close my eyes, this is where I be

Where I be is next to He, the one who created me to be

I exist in a space where I am free of those who want to control me, and what and whom I be

See I'm loud, I shout, I scream, I yell, I cuss, I fuss

But

I dream! I love!

See, I'm not one way, I'm every way, and it's there in my truth I'll stay

I cry, I'm shy, I'm soft, I'm hard, I'm rough, I'm tough

But

I'm sweet, I'm neat

It's in my truth I'll stay, and where I'll be

See, I exist because this is who I be, and how he made me

I'm uniquely unique and that's more than okay with me

I refuse to be a shell of who you think I should be

To fit in your space and place, and world that wasn't designed for me

Do you see

Do you see

Me

Do you see I'm designed to be free

Not to run with the pack

I'm strong, strong enough to let it and them leave me

As I run toward my future fate and destiny

I exist in a realm you dare not be because it was made just for me

I breathe in a space that's chemically and atomically designed for me to be

When I close my eyes this is where I be, even with people around me

See this is my place to be

My spot to be free

Where I am with thee, the one who created me to be free

Free from shame

Free from blame

Free

I have to run free

I wasn't designed to be still, meek, quiet, timid, inside or out

I need and want to turn up and shout

I need to stand in the midst of the world as its signature engulfs me, surges through me

As I am one with thee

4-28-2016

Birthing Pains

During a woman's conference at the Suitland location of my church, God gave me a vision of a woman's water breaking and her birthing pains before the service started. He reminded me of the time when a church member's water broke in our church during service. I was at church the day this took place, but I was not near her in the room where her water broke, they took her in to be comfortable until she made it to the hospital. Dr. White rushed to her side to tend to her as the pastors prayed for her and the baby. God showed her water-breaking and birthing pains to me as if I was in the room with her watching her sitting on the pastor's couch in their office.

I asked God why are you showing this to me and what am I supposed to do with it? I am asking this in my head while watching the praise team. I am literally having a visual experience with God. Remembering and seeing details that I was not there for. While having a natural experience in the earth. While asking him questions simultaneously. Sounds wild, I know! But it happened!

Apostle Carpenter preaches, the roof of the place. During her sermon, she says I see birthing pains I'm thinking, oh wow God just showed me that. My mind is blown as always by how God does that! It never stops amazing me. Later on in the service, a alter call was made where Apostle Carpenter said that this is birthing season. I did not hesitate to get to the altar. I went to the altar and stood. At that moment I began to understand what God showed me. We were asked by the Apostle to get on our knees. I dropped down to my knees. I began to pray talk to God and speak in tongues, crying the whole time.

The Apostle is praying, talking in tongues, and walking through us all laying hands on us. She touched me the first time I was still rocking back and forth with my hands up crying out and then she came back and touched me again. it was at that point that I collapsed literally screaming out to God. yelling in between screams "Jesus"! Uncontrollably! several times as if I was giving birth or having birthing pains, banging my fist on the floor as I am screaming out! I could not control any of my actions from me collapsing to me screaming. The next day I realized I had collapsed so hard that I landed on my fist and put a bruise on my chest.

God is so freaking amazing he gives you glimpses of what is to come!

The spiritual part of us is eternal the human part of us temporary!

It Was Me

It was me who messed up my life.

By not engaging in my life with me before I started adding entities to me.

It was me who didn't listen to the owls in my life who eagle-eyed.

I tried to be an owl, but was really an owlet, needing nutrients, water, and the son.

Which I thought I digested! But for more than the obvious didn't, somehow.

So, what's next more son, more water, more nutrients, more growth?

I need to be weeded from choking hazards that face me or growth is impossible.

I thought I had it. It, meaning life my life, all figured out. I thought I was on the right path.

After a few miles, I looked up and realized the path I took was so wrong and that I was so lost.

I went too far to turn back.

I soon realized that there are always detours both good and bad along the way.

A few roads I took thinking they were safe put me back on the paths I was lost on.

Others I was too afraid of the uncertainty of the terrain so I passed, but should have taken. Thinking the road less traveled was the best.

Maybe the more obstacles to overcome the better.

9-18-2009

Father In Love

The night before we commemorated/celebrated my father in loves transition to heaven, I saw him. My father-in-love was so sweet to me sarcastic as he may have been it was all love. We as a family would go to my in-law's house every other weekend to just hang out as a family. All of my husband's siblings would be there with their children. It was a happy good time. This beautiful soul would see that his son was working my nerves sometimes, and he would say come on and get a shot. He had a well-stocked bar in his basement. We would sit down and talk about any, and everything.

I would sit and tell him about the visions that I have had all of my life. He never once made me feel like I was crazy, judged me, or gave me that look of yeah, right, okay that I frequently got as a child and adult from family and friends that I would try to tell things to. I've been told throughout the years that I should never tell anyone about them. So, I became accustomed to never telling anyone about this beautiful gift god has entrusted to me, out of fear of not being believed or understood. But somehow, I felt very comfortable with sharing this side of me with him, maybe it was the alcohol! He actually engaged back with me by asking me questions and telling me stories of others he knew that had this same gift. which I loved.

The night before his funeral my mother-in-love wanted everybody to stay at the house for the next day's celebration. That night my son and I slept on the couch. Marcus was only two when his grandfather transitioned home. I was laying on the couch asleep when I just felt his presence next to me. So, I opened my eyes and there he stood all a glow, in this beautiful blue-white glowing light silent and still. With an angel on each side of him.

he looked at me I looked back at him quietly, just looking. I watched in silence as he moved from me to standing over Marcus. I watched him go and stand over each one of his grandchildren. I closed my eyes and went back to sleep. Periodically my father-in-love would pop in on me wearing his beloved black red and white kappa jacket. He would ask me if I was all right. He knew his son and I was having a hard time.

We are all spiritual beings having a human experience!

The Birds Speak

While driving and praising God soaking in his presence. Just being grateful and thankful asking him five thousand questions like I always do. I asked God since we are all one with nature can all the animals really understand us when we speak to them? I pull up to a stop sign. On my lefthand side, sat anywhere between 10 to 15 all-black birds sitting on guard rails on the corner. One bird was facing me seeming to look directly at me. The rest of them had their backs to me.

I said in full faith. Hi, birds! all the birds but the one who was looking directly at me all turned around flapped their wings about three or four times and sat back down. I was like oooh my lord did that really just happen the birds heard me and waved hi! I was so full that day and just mesmerized by God's love for the little things. Whatever you talk to him about, he hears you! he listens to you and he responds. If he can use a bird why not you?

Fear is the fruit of unbelief; Faith is the fruit of believing!

The Love of Love

The love of love
has to be the root
in all areas
of your life
you have to get in love
to get out of selfishness

Knowing God Intimately

At the women's conference, God took me on the most wonderful journey to get to know him intimately and personally. During the conference while in deep worship and prayer. God brought me to a room in heaven where he was standing. The room was a neutral tannish almost light grayish kind of color very calm, peaceful, tranquil feeling. I knew I was physically still standing at my seat at church but my soul and mind were in heaven with God. On earth, I was standing at my seat with my right leg forward and my left leg back, with my arms down and slightly back. In heaven, I was kneeling with my right leg up and my left knee down with my arms spread out and back with my head down kneeling and bowing before the king of kings.

The room we were in was empty. There were tall coulombs to the left and right looking out behind God there was nothing but darkness the floor was black and grey marble with specks of gold. There was a very wide about 8 to 10 steps stairway to the front of me. It seemed to be the same colors as the coulombs the tannish almost grayish color of the coulombs and the stairway seemed to light the room. I kneeled at the bottom of the stairway as if I knew that's where I belonged. As I was kneeling Jesus came down the stairway toward me. He spoke to me which felt like I was there for some time in his presence. I do not remember what was said I do remember how I felt. I felt honored and proud and oh so humbled. I felt submissiveness and blessed all rolled into one to be in his presence. In that moment, I knew I was chosen, called, and blessed by God to do amazing things for his kingdom. I was crowned, knighted, and blessed all in one by God. On earth, my body was still in the position, I was crying and honored.

Everyone else around me I could no longer hear. My body was there but my soul and mind were with the lord in heaven. My widows my eyes, when I opened them, would let me tap or look back into this earth realm where I saw everyone praising God. God finished talking to me. then I came back fully into the sanctuary in the midst of everyone praising and worshiping. I am sure my soul absorbed every bit of knowledge and wisdom the lord bestowed upon me. I remember that it amazed me that God moves his hands and arms when he talks just like people do. Looking back on when I wrote this down, I know that we are made in his image so of course, we would mimic our maker when we talk. God wore a tan or cream-colored long garment with a hood on his head deep enough so I never saw his face. Only his hands and feet.

Now that I am fully back in the sanctuary I continue to praise and worship. A few moments later I was told by God to look up. When I looked up the ceiling was gone. There was this bright beautiful blue sky with fluffy white clouds. Just very breathtakingly beautiful. As I was watching the sky, I began to see for a second what I thought were white birds as they got closer, I knew they were angels one by one they flew in. Dancing in the sky till there were hundreds flying so delicately and intricately in beautiful patterns in Unisom. At one point I noticed I was moving my hands in the same patterns the angels were flying and dancing in. I don't know if I was following them or if they were following me. Either way, I was nothing but blessed and truly honored to witness this miraculous event unfold before me. The angels began to fly in a circle, hundreds and hundreds of angels flying in this wide and deep beautiful circle. The clouds in the sky dissipated as the angels bow their heads while still flying in the circle. God himself begins to descend down this heavenly angel tunnel straight into the sanctuary.

God begins to walk down the aisle to my right. He stops by someone I feel led to pray, and I extend my arm on that side. He stays for a moment and then moves on to another person. I feel led to pray for them as well, I extend my hand on that side. In the natural, my body is still facing forward but my head turns in whichever direction my lord moves. I'm following him throughout the sanctuary. I am extending my arm and hand to whichever side of me he is on praying for whomever he is loving, healing, and changing lives on. He traveled to several people all around the sanctuary and each time I did the same.

I am now back listening to the speaker of the conference. I begin to look around like where are you now? He says beside you. I look to my right and there my God was! In the natural, we were standing person beside-person in the conference. My body is still and facing forward. In the supernatural, my soul was literally jumping up and down like a kid in a candy store super excited. I asked God, what's going on God? He said I came to give everyone what they needed. In my head, for a split second, I'm thinking but your right here how are you going to do that? He told me to look to the left. I did! He was standing right beside me. But I knew he was right there for the lady that was to my left, not me. He never left my side. God that was for me standing to the right of me.

I looked around the entire sanctuary God was literally standing next to every single person in the room. For Some people he was bent over, for some he was kneeling for others he was holding and touching. I looked to my right where God was standing for me. I'm in complete amazement. God said I am here to give everyone what they need. What I felt I needed was answers to a question that I had been wondering about for quite some time. As well as physical love, attention, and affection. God stretched out his arms and hugged me so gently and tight. He let me know that he loved me and never forgot about me. God let me know that he will always be there for me. My embrace with God felt like a lifetime. I never wanted to let go! I was so full of glee. I just smiled at the love. God let me go but stood there. I interlocked my arm with his and laid my head on his shoulder with such elation and freedom as if I just knew I could do that. I was so filled with love. What probably lasted seconds in the natural was an eternity in the supernatural.

The question that I have been asking God, was how can one person see one thing and another person see something completely different at the same time. God was showing me and answering my questions at the same time while giving me my heart's desire. For those of you who don't know me. God knows I need to know the complete nuts and bolts and screws of a situation the fabric and the texture of it all to get it. I am a, you have to show me kind of girl for me to understand it. God said while my head was laid on his shoulder, "I came to give them what they needed while I'm giving you what you need." God said! "I'm God I'm omnipresent!" I never really knew or understood what that really meant till that very moment. The speaker (Apostle Cynthia Brazelton) began to speak about the mighty presence of God the room erupted with praise wells and cries thanking God for his love. I was completely immersed back into the service after that.

That following Sunday in church Pastor Portia began to speak on the mighty move of God that took place at this conference. She said please come to the altar please share looking dead straight in my direction which felt like at me. I was still sitting in my seat. There were people standing all around the altar worshiping Pastor Portia looked my way with just a glance and said with authority there are those of you who are sitting when you know you need to come share. At that moment I knew she was talking to me I knew I needed to go share what God showed me. As I walked to the altar through the crowd, she held out the mic toward me and said I was waiting for you to come share. I was trembling from my head to my toes. I shared what god allowed me to see as well as a previous vision. While typing this I realized I did not share in full detail as I am now of my encounter with God and what I was shown.

After I was done delivering the message several women came over to me at the altar and told me, thank you for sharing. I nodded my head still shock that I was even up there and said thank you. One lady told me she was one of the ones God came to and you prayed for me! she said thank you! I said you are welcome. After service, a senior member come up to me and said thank you for confirming what I saw. I thought I made it up or I wasn't sure if it was real. Thank you again, she said. I said you're welcome and hugged her. Several other church members and elders came up to me: Darlena Austin whom I will forever be overly grateful. She introduced me to my church home and Decan Robyn both said to me don't hide your gift from God from the world. The world needs you to walk in your full gift from God.

It took me so long to type these encounters out even though I was typing it from my journal that I wrote out years ago. Re-reading it I remembered and re-felt every single emotion all over again as if I was reliving it. I had to keep stopping to cry and to get myself together. I'm just in awe of his love every step of the way.

Having, true faith is when you believe, just believe! No plan B!

My Love Letter

You saw through the façade I had on display of me

Straight to my heart that I betrayed in foolish haste of me

You saw my spirit that should have been on display for all to see

Just how your eternal love has taught me to be free of me

You love me despite of me

You protected me despite of me

You lead me through the fire without a singe to be seen

You lead me through

You lead me through

You lead me through

I Love You, I Love You, I Love You

I am free, I am free, I am free

To be

Because of you and how you loved me

You alone held my hand, pulled me through, shielded me, covered me, hovered over me

From those who tried to kill me, destroy me, take me away from thee

Your grace and your mercy

Saved me, saved me, saved me

I am free to be

because of thee

And how you first loved me

When God Shows You What To Wear

My cousin's father and my childhood friend went home to heaven suddenly. Her father and I always kept in touch through the years. He loved to tell me about all my cousin RaeJean's accomplishments. I was more than eager to know how well she was doing. Going to his funeral was important to me. I wanted to make sure I was there for her and to honor him. The night before the funeral I was going over options of what to wear. At this point in life, I refuse to wear black to another funeral. I had the top I wanted to wear in mind and set it aside in my closet. I looked at a gold pair of paints, and a grey pair. I could not figure it out. So, I decided to just go to sleep and choose in the morning.

While sleeping God showed me exactly what to wear. In my vision, God showed me walking to the closet. I opened the door. The white shirt that I had already chosen and a pair of red capri pants were held up and out as if someone was holding them still on the hangers. I remember thinking that this is perfect. It will work! Yes! Okay, God! The next thing I know it was time for me to wake up. I got up and went straight to my closet to get the clothes that God chose for me. I got myself together and headed straight to the funeral.

At the funeral, I noticed that my cousin Lita RaeJean's Mom, James's family, and everybody that knew him well all wore red. His flowers were also red and white. My mouth dang near hit the floor. I just looked around in amazement like God you are so good! I always say God how do you do that in shock every time. It's God he can do all things! During the funeral, God showed me a small glimpse of James (Foxxy) dressed in all white walking down the center aisle toward his daughter, and just that fast my vision of him was gone. I love when God allows me to see. God truly does care about every aspect of us even after we have gone home to be with him. His omnipotent love for us is life-changing special and sweet.

6-1-2022

Direct your focus onto the lord and he will direct your life!

I

I live in a place of love

I exist in a space that's free

I breathe in a realm that's inhabited by thee

I see in a land that's bright

I talk in an atmosphere that's me

I dance on a journey that's gleaming

I sing in a world that's filled with glee

I touch in a galaxy that's anatomically designed just for me to be

6-1-2015

When God Speaks At Funerals

My great aunt Juanita passed away a few years ago. She was named for her mother Juanita Hilda Turner my Great Grandmother. My Aunt Juanita was nicknamed Baby Sis, then shortened to BaSis. She was the gentlest of souls. Kind-hearted and so sweet to everyone. She could make the best-fried potatoes and onions I have ever had. I truly love my great Auntie. I remember when I was a child, one summer I was going to vacation bible school camp. I made a ceramic arc I painted and glazed it. I was so proud of myself and so overly excited to show her what I had made. She asked me if she could keep it. I was so happy and elated that she wanted it. She kept it for years. I would look forward to seeing it every time we visited her house. She kept my masterpiece in the living room on the TV stand. I vividly remember the sense of feeling so much pride that I made that and that she wanted it on display for all to see.

I was more than happy and honored when her oldest child Ronald asked me to read her eulogy. This was one of the few times, I was not overly nervous to stand in front of a sea of people and actually speak. I read her eulogy with pride and honor. I read over the eulogy several times to myself, before stepping to the podium it all seemed right. While reading the eulogy I get to the very last line where it's naming her favorite things to do. I hear God say "puzzle" loud and clear so I immediately say puzzles and then finish the sentences. I look up at my family and see her son and daughter-in-law and she says Ohh My God how did I forget that? Everyone at the funeral was nodding their heads and saying yes it was. As a child, she would always have a puzzle on the dining room table that she would walk over to and put a piece in as if she knew exactly where they went. Auntie would let me try when

I was little. I don't think I ever once got a piece in place. She would tell me puzzles took patience. God cares about you and your legacy. He never forgets about you and what you love. If you are one and in tune with God, he will talk to you. God only needed to say one word to remind everyone of what was missing to complete the puzzle.

Be one with God so that everything that comes out of your mouth is of him!

Live

I live in a world where I dare to be

Just to be

Just to see

If I can be

I live out loud in a world where I dare to be

Daring you to try me

I live free in a world that tries to hold me

Control me

But

I control this world that holds me

And

Consoles me

2-2-2016

Double Dose Vision

During a powerful Sunday service where Pastor Demond was preaching about being the light of the earth and how light always illuminates reveals and exposes. Light discovers. I looked to the left and saw an army standing in the aisle way. They were dressed in all green and standing at attention facing the altar as if they were waiting to receive orders. Just as fast as I saw them there, I was brought back to this natural realm.

The service commenced a few moments later, Pastor Portia made an altar call for the youth to come to the altar to get prayed for, and she began praying for all the youth in Charles County. As she began to pray, I was led to look up and saw that there was an open portal above the church showing a beautiful blue sky with white fluffy clouds as she prayed golden light rings shot outward across the county over and over and over to the youth in the county.

Don't think about it Just believe!

Face Book Face Look

I hold my destiny in my hands

My fate and future lie in me looking to thee

To determine where I'll be

I'll stand strong in thee

who stands for me

In my future

I claim as my own

With the one who sits high on the throne

To guide and protect

Let's never forget
To worship thee in all that he be

11-9-2022

Crashing Waves

I love you, Jesus, I worship and adore you, I just want to tell you lord that I love you more than anything!

Like a rushing wave, I'm causing everything to change!

This Sunday's service was a full praise and worship service. While praising God and thanking him I looked up to the heavens. God showed me that the ceiling of the sanctuary had a hole. The hole just kept spinning as if it was a propeller blade or an industrial fan blade spinning. I was like ok lord I don't understand it but I pressed in still praising still worshipping. Speaking in my holy faith thanking him for all he does. The next image was of a still wave not moving just frozen in time. I am still pressing in still praising, still speaking in tongues. the wave is under the moving propeller blade. I am still like ok God, so I continue to keep pressing in.

Pastor Demond has an altar call for healing I go to the altar. He places his hands on me for healing I collapse to the floor still seeing the propeller above me. I get up and go tell Minster Halliburton what I saw, she tells me to tell Minister Tyrone who is assisting Pastor Demond. So, I go do just that. Pastor Demond explains how God has been showing him an industrial fan all week that was not moving. Minister Haliburton comes over to me standing at my seat puts her arm around me and says did you hear that? I say yes! She says God is using you. I broke out shouting, clinging on to her, crying, praising, and speaking in tongues uncontrollably. Like a crashing wave, he's causing everything to change. I remand at my seat God continued to show me more.

The wave floods us all in the sanctuary. I watched the water flow from the front to the back as if it was blessing everyone's feet it touched. We are all standing in inches of water. I keep looking at my feet. I can see the carpet in the church through the water. the water was crystal clear. I keep stomping my feet in the water. While the praise team is singing like a rushing wave, I'm causing everything to change over and over. In the natural, I am speaking in tongues thanking God, and waving my hands back and forth in the direction of the wave and the flow of water flowing through the sanctuary from front to back. I went from using my left hand and then my right I am praying for the people as the water touches their feet.

I love you, Jesus, I worship and adore you, I just want to tell you lord that I love you more than anything!

Like a rushing wave, he's causing everything to change!

Stay in faith to receive your blessings!

I Am

I am

Because I have always been

A Queen

A Dream

A Fein

Because I am that bad that mean

That chic that lives and loves

If you want to know me listen to my muse

My muse is my music

My music is my essence

My essence is my soul

1-1-2012

Apostle Tony preached and made an altar call for all the Pastors to come down to be prayed for. All the pastors came to the front. The Apostles began to pray over each leader as the leaders began to be slain in the spirit and fell to their knees God showed me a vision that came down from the heavens like a projections screen. Showing me the spiritual/supernatural family lineage of his word from the heavens to the earth. God, Apostles, Pastors, Ministers, Congregation, Family, and the World. God showed me a flood-down effect.

After the service was over, I saw Apostle Tony in the foyer of the church. I hugged him which was amazing in itself as if I was with family and oracle all rolled into one. I explained to him the vision God gave me as he was praying over the pastors, he said that was God. I explained that I also saw the pandemic before it came and did not understand what I was seeing. I talked to him about how Pastor Portia told me it was time for me to get in position, in and for God. He said so you are a seer. I said yes. I then said I have to be so intentional about what I watch and hear. He said yes you do! And if you don't you will be of no use to God.

That hit me like a megaton of bricks. No use to God! What! There is no way I'm going to willingly give up on such a tremendous responsibility and gift, for this world and my own doing. I love what God is calling out of me. Living in the world by any means, muddles and dulls my sensitivity to God and his word. It's nothing but a distraction of the enemy to keep me and you from the calling God has on our lives. This to me is the very definition of die to your flesh to receive everything that the father has for you.

Those of us who use food, drugs, sex, money, etc. We think the issue is that it is not. It's your disconnect from that which is real, which is God. You keep trying to feed yourself with what cannot sustain you. Instead of facing the real issues you disconnect from the source and numb out!

Where Does Your Allegiance Lie

Apostle Hope came and blessed the Virtuous Women's Conference with a powerful message. Do you know who you are in Christ? Are you walking in your victory? What does heaven say about everything that you do? Those three points right there took me to another place and level. She followed that with are you willing to lose people to walk out of this faith and what's in this book. You can't hang out with just anybody when you are walking out this life. You have to be intentional. I have to be intentional in everything I do! Who you are around, what you watch, and read, what and whom you listen to, and what you do. It all matters. Are you willing to pay the price?! I have been straddling the fence far too long. The line has been drawn in the sand and I'm stepping across it. No turning back!

Apostle Hope asked a question is your flesh fighting with your spirit? I wanted to scream YES! She made an altar call for the women to come down to get prayed for. But I never got out of my seat knowing good and darn well I needed to get prayed for. God showed me something so magical and wonderful as Apostle Hope was praying and laying hands on the women. God showed me blue-ish white glowing orbs coming through the entrance doors to the sanctuary rushing down the aisles making their way to the altar where the Apostle was still standing laying hands and praying for everyone. Each orb that flooded the altar then went to a person in the sanctuary. Each orb began to glow at different intensity levels according to the person it belonged to. Some of the people's orb lights were dim and small, and some of the women's lights glowed small and a little brighter. I looked down in front of me, my orb light felt hazy. I saw the glow but where was my intensity in my shine? I could see straight through it.

I looked over toward Apostle Hope her orb glowed so big and bright that I could not see the person she was praying for or some of the people around her. I could only see the top and back of her head. As I looked around the room the orb lights were of all intensities different with each person as if it was tied to your level of belief, love, and trust in and for God. You have to know, that you know, that you know that God got you! Walk in that, trust in that. Live in that and out of that place! No turning back! I want my light to shine so brightly to the world that it is undeniable to whom I serve! And whom I belong to! I want it to be a beacon to the world to whom I pledge my allegiance to! The question is whom do you pledge yours to? Is it yourself, this world, or God?!

We often block our blessings because we don't feel worthy enough. You are worthy enough because you are born and here. You must have an alignment of your heart and faith!

Love Loves Me

God is/= Love

Love

Loves Me

And because

Love

Loves me

I have nothing but Love

To give back to my Love

Love is why

I am here

Giving my Love back to Love

Loving my Love

Who loves me

Fills my heart with love for thee

2-14-2003